This Book Belongs to:

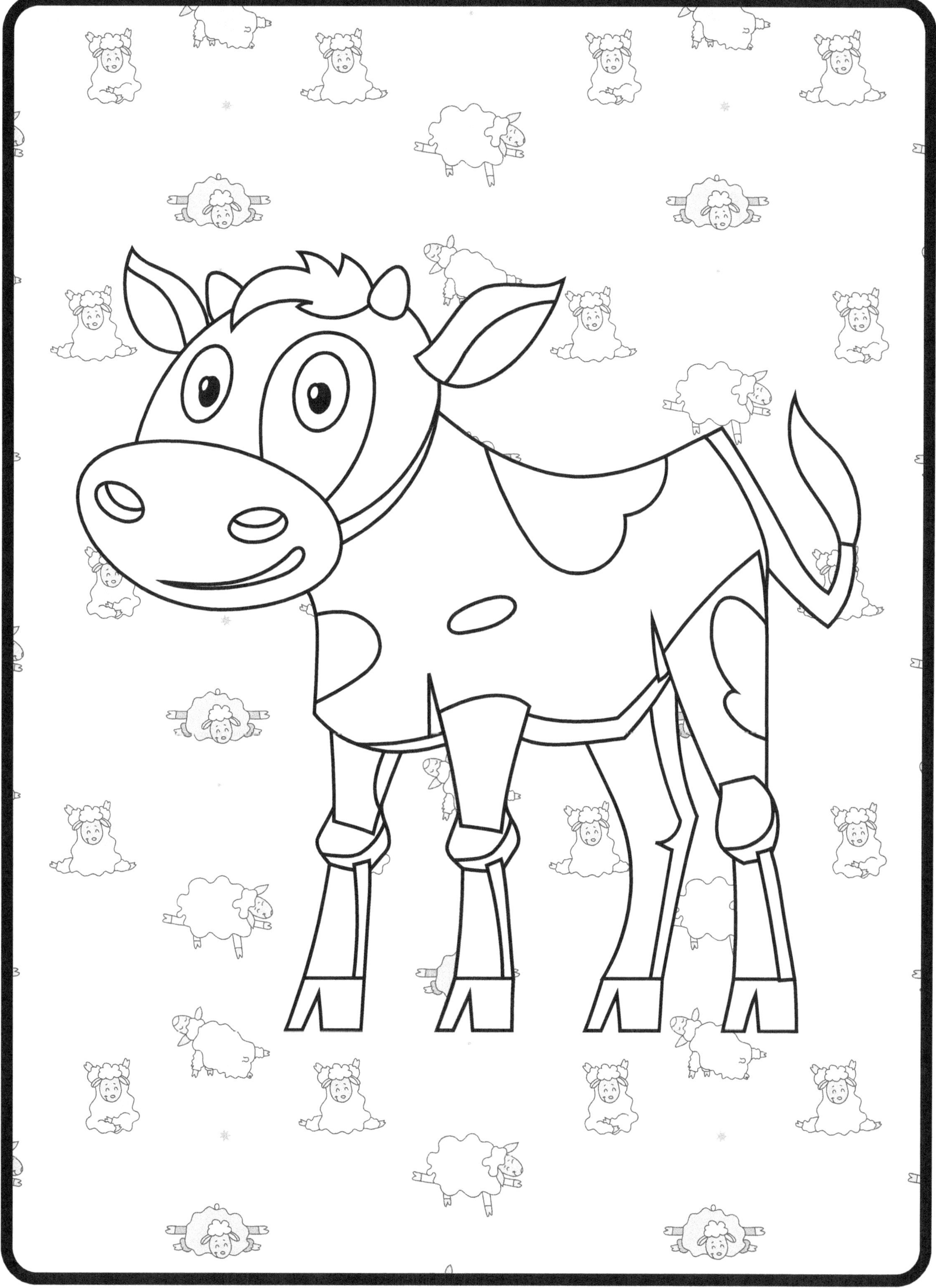

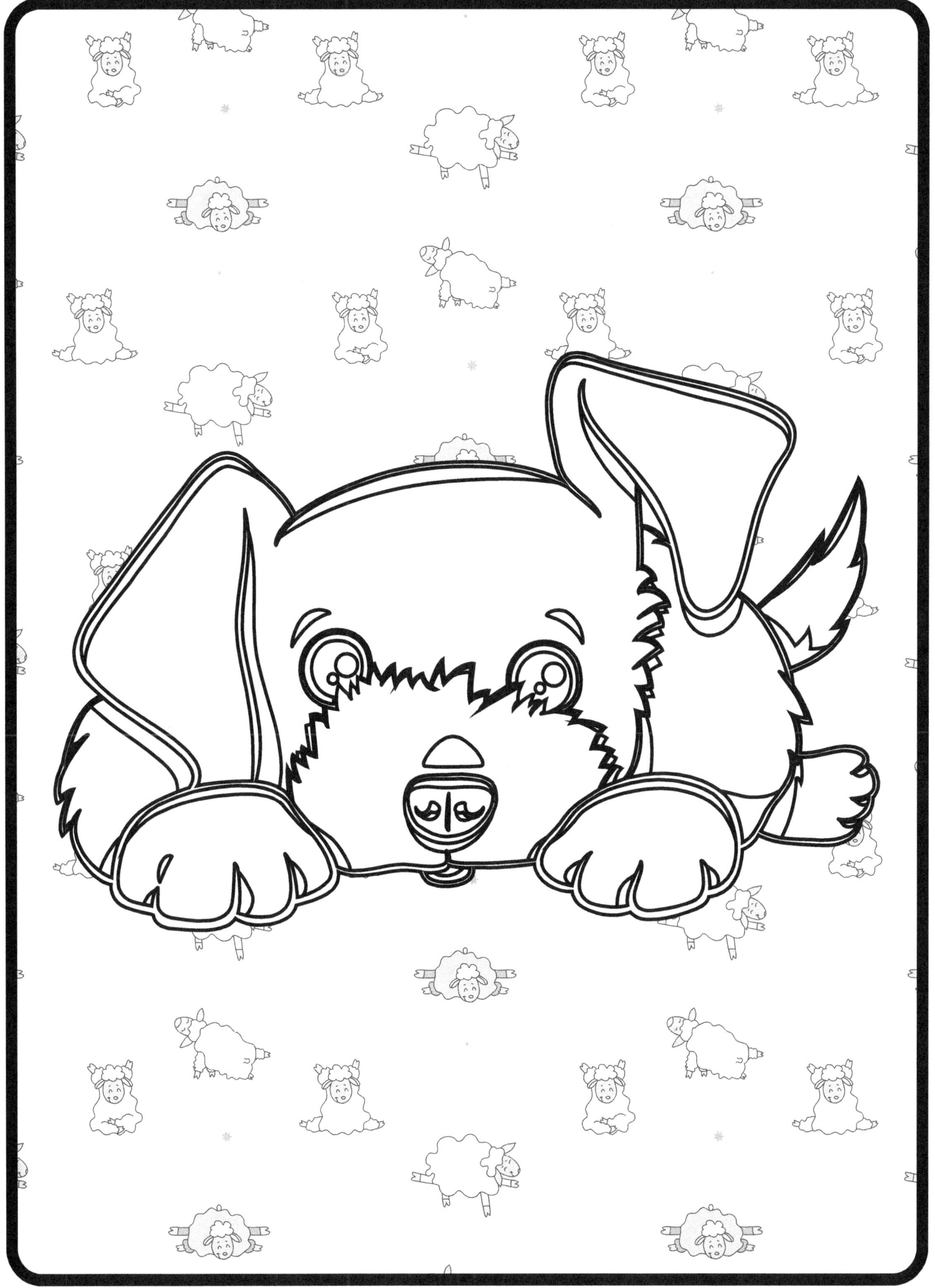

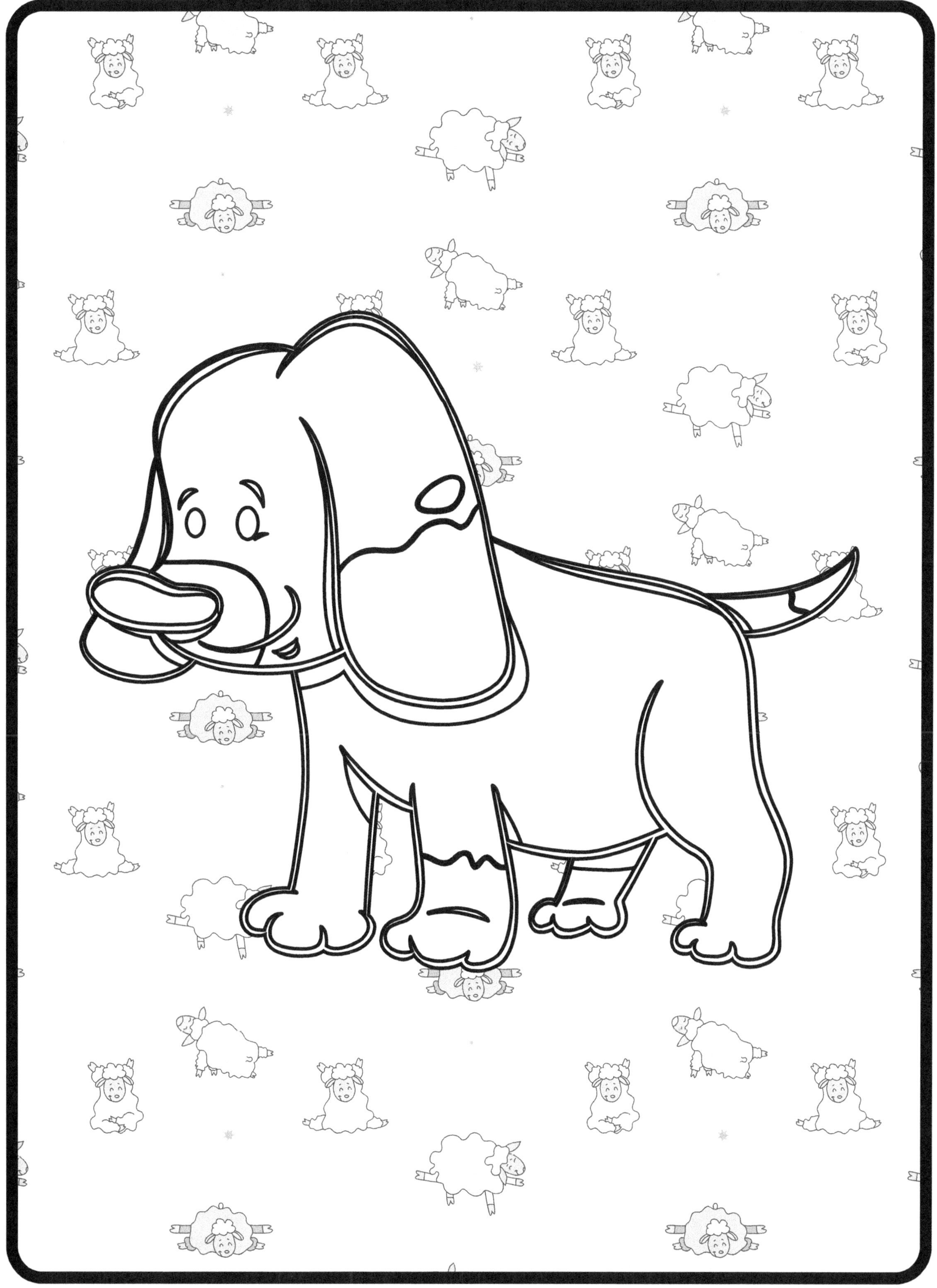

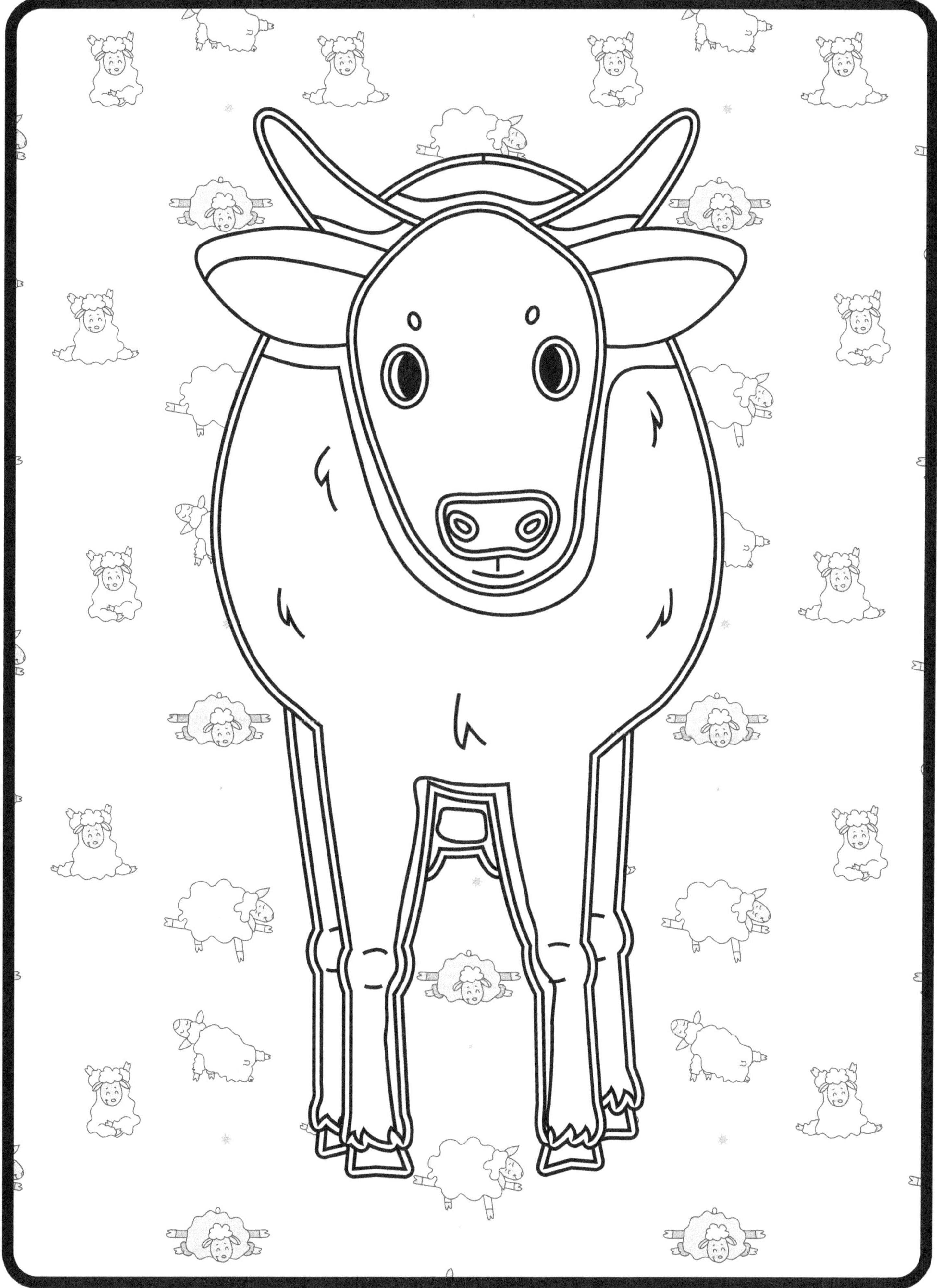

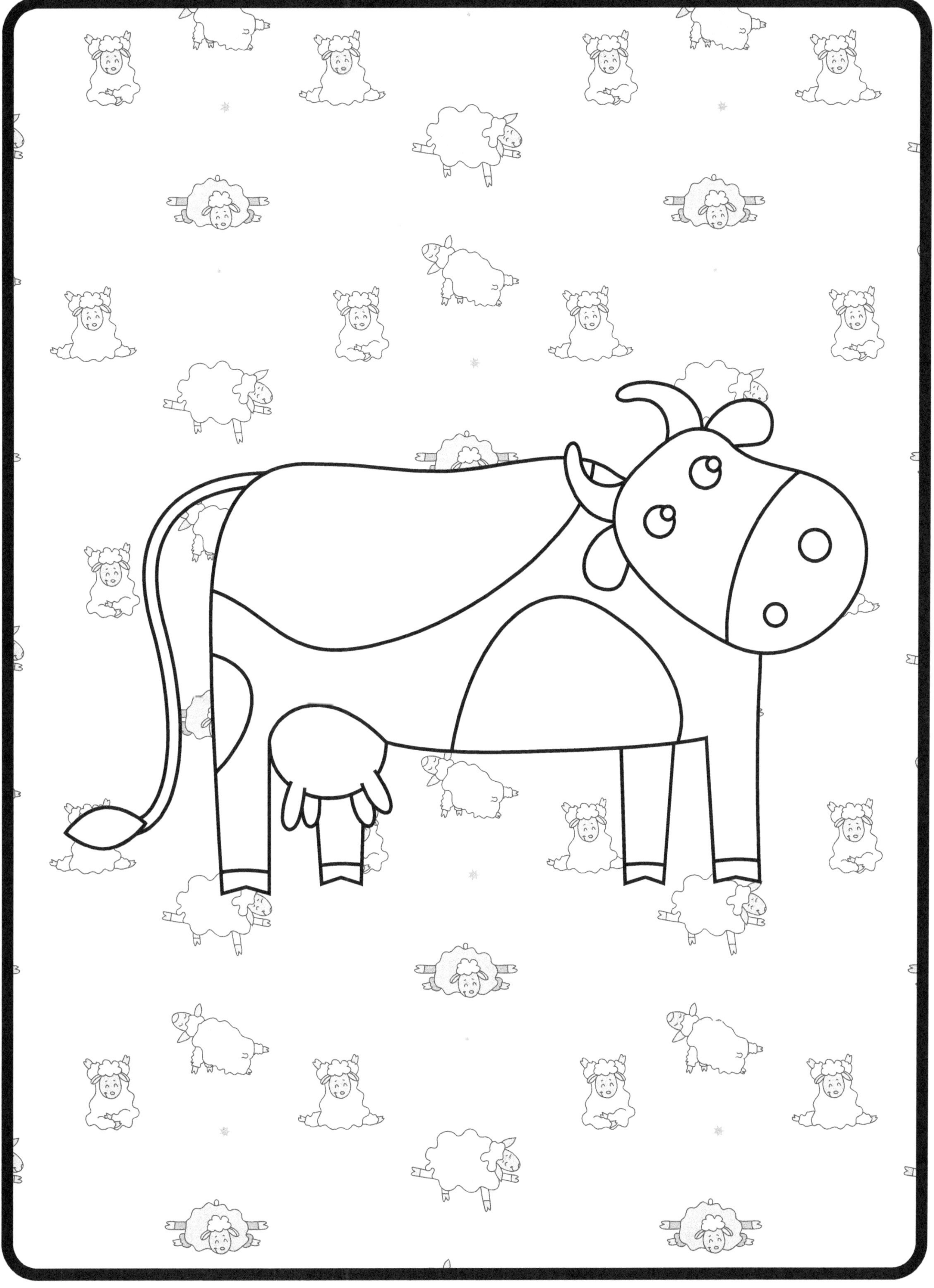

Hello!

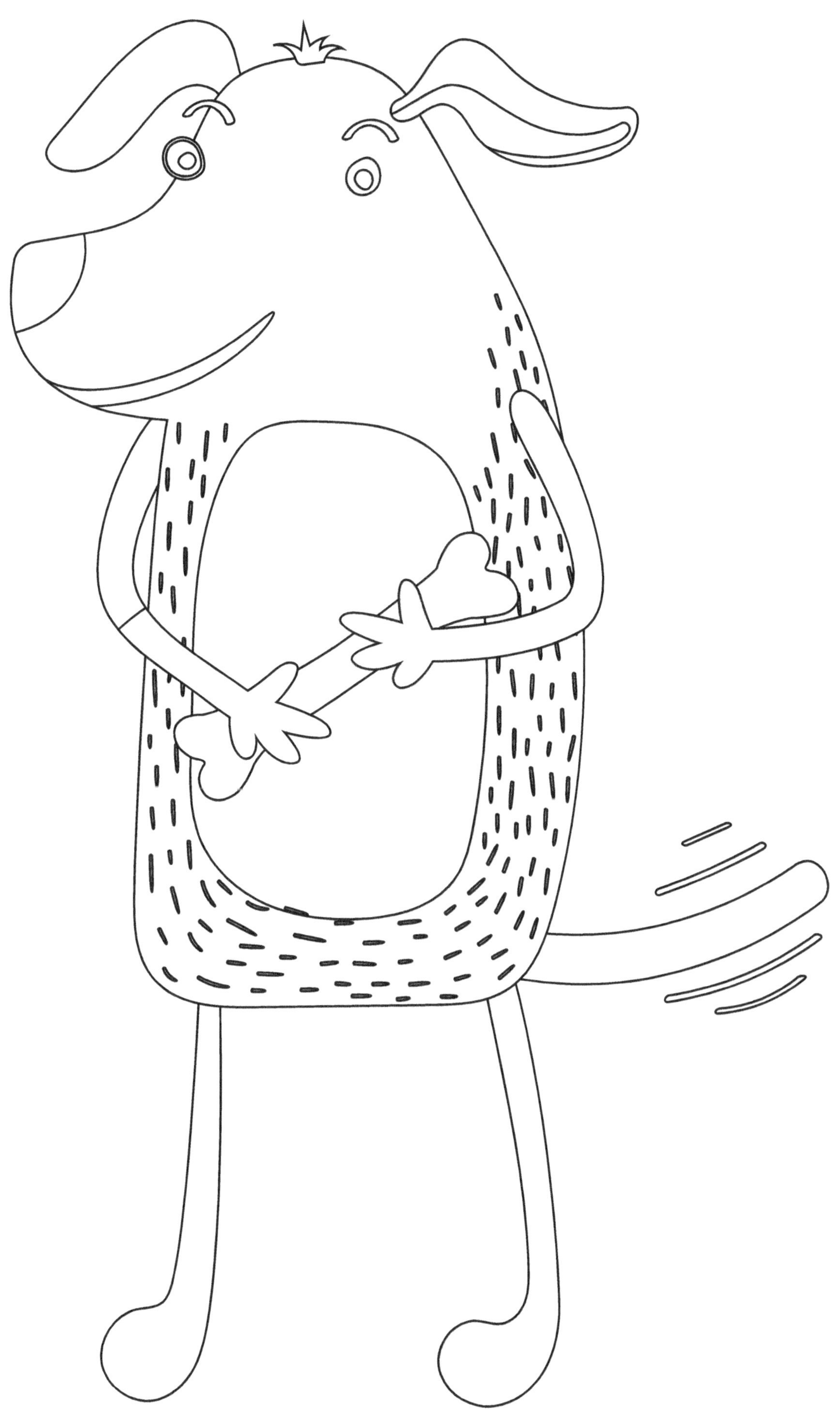

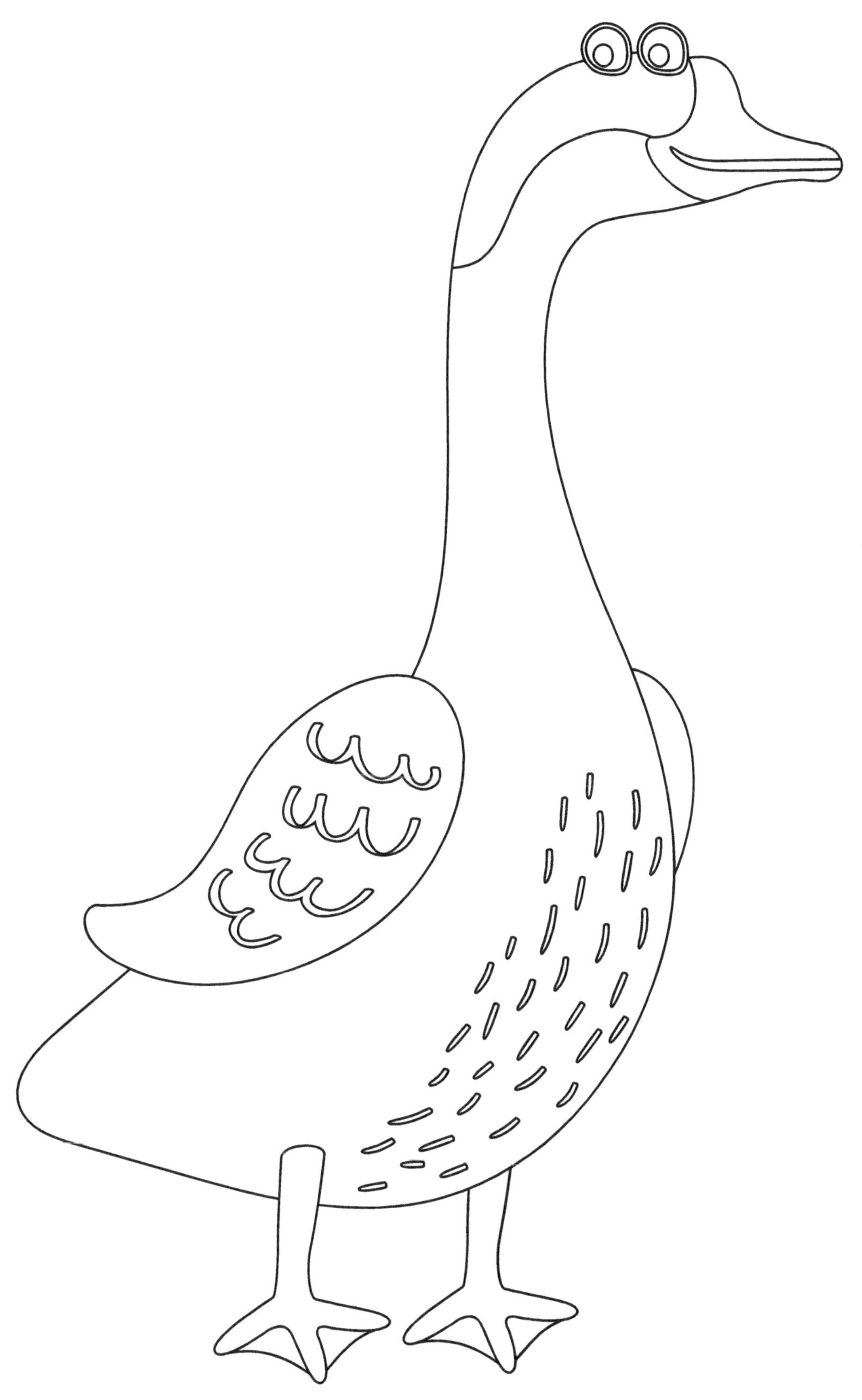